WHEN
DEATH
DRAWS
NEAR

WHEN DEATH DRAWS NEAR

PHILIP W. WILLIAMS

AUGSBURG Publishing House • Minneapolis

WHEN DEATH DRAWS NEAR

Copyright © 1979 Augsburg Publishing House

Library of Congress Catalog Card No. 78-66945

International Standard Book No. 0-8066-1694-6

Scripture quotations unless otherwise noted are from the Re-
vised Standard Version of the Bible, copyright 1946, 1952,
and 1971 by the Division of Christian Education of the National Council of Churches. Quotations from Today's English
Version (TEV) copyright 1976 by American Bible Society.
Quotations from the Jerusalem Bible (JB) copyright 1966 by
Doubleday and Co., Inc.

The quotation from *Free Fall* by JoAnn Kelley Smith, copyright 1975 by Judson Press, is used by permission of the pub-
lisher.

Cover design: Wendell Mathews

Cover photo: New Light, Inc.—Marc Shoemaker

Other photos: J. Bruce Baumann/Image, page 26; Philip Gen-
dreau, 36; Camerique, 46; Wallowitch, 54, 68; A. Devaney,
Inc., 62; *Lutheran Standard,* 76; Paul M. Schrock, 86; Vivienne,
94.

To my father and mother
and in memory
of "Pa"

contents

introduction

A startling statement is sometimes made by people who are dying: "I never knew what it was to live until I had to face my own dying!"

That statement is hard for me to understand. Sure, I can say, like hundreds upon hundreds of other people, "I'm dying every day," but that is a removed, philosophical statement that doesn't hit my heart. I acknowledge that I'm losing brain cells, I'm growing bald, I can't run as fast, I forget more easily. Yet I don't know what dying is all about until I'm in it.

Being "in it" is hearing, "You have cancer. We'll do all we can to help you." Being "in it" is hearing, "You've had a massive coronary. Your heart is severely damaged, but with care, you *may* be all right." Being "in it" is hearing, "The physical damage has gone too far. We haven't given up though. We'll keep trying, and we'll keep you as comfortable as we can." However you and I hear it, however it is said, now we know we are the persons who are, in fact, dying.

When this reality hits us, many things happen. Some of us question God's goodness. This merciful God I believe in now allows or causes or permits or wants me to die! What is the worth of faith if ultimately I am to die? We might think that we shouldn't have such thoughts. Weren't we raised to not question God's wisdom and control? That may be! Yet it is not unchristian to wonder and ask, particularly when I am the one who is dying. And questions often enter the minds of relatives and friends.

Questioning isn't abnormal or wrong. In fact, it can be expected in most Christian people. The issue isn't whether we ought to think and feel this way or not. The issue is whether we can allow ourselves this painful wondering, and then move on. We need to work through our questions, using the resources within ourselves and within our Christian tradition and faith.

It is to this questioning and the need to find support, understanding, and meaning in dying that these meditations are directed. We will share the experiences of others, some of which may be similar to yours. Each of us is unique, even peculiar. Yet, among us dying people and among our relatives and friends, there is an uncommon commonality of feelings, attitudes, and experiences. We learn to depend on one another.

Through it all, each of us is embraced by a Lord who knows, hurts, suffers, celebrates, and cares for us. He died and rose to give us his eternal gift of life. He gave us the real hope that in our dying, we live.

denial

It Can't Be True!

When I was a tyke, one of the many stories my grandmother read to me was "The Little Red Hen." Naturally, my children now have this childhood classic in their tattered and torn library. Remember how the cat, pig, and duck kept refusing to help the little red hen? They wouldn't plant, nourish, or reap the grain. They wouldn't prepare and bake the bread. Their familiar refrain was always, "Not I!" When the bread was baked, fresh and hot out of the oven, ready to eat, they all suddenly changed their tune. None of them wanted any part of the preparation, yet they all wanted a slice of the delicious final product. They were disappointed when the hen ate the bread herself.

Sometimes, like the cat, the pig, and the duck, you and I refuse to be part of the process

12

and we deny responsibility for what is happening. The results of refusal and putting off and denial are often like the story says. We can't claim the final product because we haven't put anything into the process.

When I asked Mary Lou how sick she was, she answered, "I have cancer, but I'm going to be all right." This wasn't the usual realistic and necessary hope of a sick person, but a hope loaded with denial. Mary Lou only had a few weeks to live. Yet she firmly believed she wouldn't die. She refused to take part in the process of her own dying. As a result, she denied herself the opportunity to find the sense of resolution and peace of mind that preparing for one's death can bring.

Denial is both friend and foe. As a handy defense, it helps us when we need something to stand between us and the penetrating shock of news that is too much for us to take and comprehend. Yet if it stays there and stays there like a wall too high to climb, it becomes a barrier that even God can't penetrate. We have the power to shut out truth.

To be confronted with the fact that I am dying is overwhelming. I can't help but go numb and deny it. But in time I can also help myself move on, past the numbness. Denial may sneak back at times, but without the power it once had.

Bill told his pastor, "Don't say anything to my wife and children, but I don't think I have long to live." His wife and children said, "Don't tell Bill, but we know he doesn't have long to live." All knew the truth, but they lived in fear that someone would slip up and let it out. They denied it to one another, feeling they were sparing the others. In truth, they were sparing themselves. They were also denying themselves the comfort they might have been for one another. The truth may hurt, but it also sets free.

Denial is natural, but if we are to experience support and meaning in our dying, in time we need to move on. God is ready to strengthen us, to help us accept our dying and, through acceptance, find peace.

Read Matthew 16:21-23
         Psalm 18:1-6

Dear God, sometimes I'm afraid of the truth.
It hurts, and I wonder if I'll get over it.
Help me find relief from the hurt. Help me
discover that by wrestling with the truth,
I will find it, or it will find me. In Jesus' name.
Amen.

anger

?X?!TX!

"Why, why, why?"

"Hey, if I were 75, maybe. But I'm 43, just at the peak of my work, the prime of my life! No! ?X?!TX!, God!"

"Some people think, because I'm old, I'm ready to die. Are you kidding? If I've got a few years left, I want them."

Most dying people feel fierce anger. Is my dying worth my anger? Absolutely! Life and living are precious to me. Now my job, hobbies, hopes, memories, and dreams are threatened, coming to an end. My family and friends are slipping away from me. I am being robbed of my human connections. They will go on, I won't! Who could keep a smile on his face and a lilt in his voice in the face of such loss?

We may have been taught never to be angry,

but is that realistic? Even people who say they don't get angry (they're right, they don't get angry) can't stop their angry feelings. They may not show their anger, but it's there.

Anger can be used inappropriately or destructively, but feeling angry isn't wrong. In the Garden of Gethsemane, Jesus asked his disciples to wait at a distance while he prayed. When he came back, he found them sleeping. He asked, "Could you not watch one hour?" I imagine he was not only sad, but angry.

Certainly few of us have been encouraged to be angry at God. Heaven forbid! But many dying people long to shake their fist at God and scream, "This isn't fair!" And there is no safer person to direct our anger at than our Father God.

Annie said, "I've had my bouts with anger. Why should this happen to me? I've led a pretty good life. I deserve better than this. I remember the minister preaching that being good doesn't give us a guarantee against problems and death. I heard it, but I guess I thought I was the exception. I think—God, this isn't fair! Then I ask myself, 'Well, why shouldn't it be this way? We all have to die sometime'. . . but not now! Sometimes what gets me is that, when I'm feeling angry, my people act like they don't feel it too. Maybe they do, but they don't act like it. I get angry at

17

them. I get angry at the nurses, doctors, aides, even my pastor."

In facing his death, Jesus felt the anger that comes from feeling abandoned. He not only felt anger—he dared to express it.

Like Jesus, we cry out. Our voices express the fear of loss, the loneliness of separation, the pain of the body, and the need to find meaning and saving hope. Our Lord hears, understands, and comforts.

Read Psalm 4:1-4
        Psalm 6:1-5
        Ecclesiastes 1:1-4
        Mark 14:32-42

Dear Father, I don't just feel righteously indignant—I'm angry! But I believe, good Father, that you understand me and my anger. My anger doesn't stop your loving me. Father, thank you. Amen.

bargaining
Tit for Tat

At 45, Margaret was the picture of good, solid human stock. She was a warm and protective mother and wife, yet she could command respect—you'd toe the mark. Most important, through all her qualities, she made you feel that she would love you, no matter what.

Her Christian faith was simple and strong. It was uncomplicated, but deep. She wasn't so naive that she didn't recognize life's hurts and contradictions, but for her it was enough to know that God loved her and she loved God. Even though she was dying, she always seemed a pillar of faith and strength.

One evening she confided, "I know I'm dying, but if God would let me live just long enough to see my son get married. . . ." What's this? This tower of faith and strength was bargaining with Almighty God! She was telling him that she would be willing to die if he'd postpone it a bit.

Margaret did live to see her son married. But was one bargain enough? No. Next, she asked to live long enough to see her daughter graduate from high school. Margaret died before this wish could be fulfilled.

Here was a good Christian woman bargaining with God for her life. Was she wrong? No! She was real and honest. Her life was built around her relationships, particularly to her family. She didn't want to lose out on the joys and sorrows of those relationships. She knew that someday she would. The God who loved her and whom she loved would, as Margaret said, "Call me home to heaven." But, please, not just yet. . . .

Margaret was laying out her wishes and dreams before God. But she didn't follow through on her unspoken end of the bargain. She wasn't willing to die after she saw her son married. In fact, she continued her struggle and dared to ask more! Was Margaret then to be rejected by God?

Scripture portrays good, God-fearing people who dared to bargain with God. Moses bargained, and Jacob wrestled with the angel, perhaps God himself. Peter was known to strike a bargain or two. This is real and human. God will not reject us for it.

In her real and honest way, as her disease got progressively worse, Margaret eventually stopped bargaining. As death approached, she moved from bargaining to focusing on the precious moments she had with the family and people she loved. Margaret accepted her death. She died with these words, "Love and take care of each other. I'm with God. I love you."

Read Psalm 44:14-26
        Psalm 31

*"Now I lay me down to sleep. I pray thee,
Lord, my soul to keep. If I should die before
I wake, I pray thee, Lord, my soul to take."
Sometimes this sounds childish and corny.
It's not. Watch over me, Lord. Amen.*

depression

Down in the Valley

Dick was an active, energetic man. The limitations he experienced in his dying made him feel less than the man he believed he was. His protest was a sullen, isolating depression. People didn't want to be around him. He didn't want people. He was dying slowly and miserably.

All the dying persons I have met at some time experience the downward slide into depression. Even pillars of faith, even positive thinkers who like to make us believe they have overcome sadness, "a smile on their face for the whole human race," even they, in the privacy of their own worlds, sometimes despair. It is unavoidable.

O Lord, my defender, I call to you.
Listen to my cry!

If you do not answer me,
I will be among those who go down
to the world of the dead (Ps. 128:1 TEV).

Here we read and feel the desperation of depression.

There is a dryness of the soul as one enters a wilderness. Life begins to feel empty. It loses its zest. Nothing much seems to matter. Oh, we may think that it would be nice for life to taste good again, but that passing thought is quickly buried. Besides, we don't feel we have the energy to make it any different. Who cares!

Arlene didn't. "What's the use? I wish people would leave me alone. I'm going to die. I just wish it were over." Arlene appeared to have given up. At that time, she had. But she came to see that the cloud of depression she felt hovering over her and the wilderness she felt within her were normal reactions, and that they would pass. It took time for the dark cloud to move on and the dry wilderness to be watered. But after talking to others, she confronted her depression and moved toward accepting it.

Some need medication to help remove depression. For Arlene, it helped simply to talk. She began to evaluate her feelings and thoughts about dying. She determined what was really important to her, and her attitude changed. She took quite a step—from someone who saw only the finality of death to someone who saw herself as "living unto death." Dying can be as meaningful as other stages of life for those who travel beyond the wilderness of depression.

Angie said, "When I'm depressed, I try to think of others ahead of myself. Jesus thought of others when he was dying. Even though he was hanging on a cross, he asked that his enemies be forgiven, and he made sure his mother would be taken care of. When I do something or say something nice for someone else, I feel better myself."

But, like so many other feelings and conditions, depression can't be left behind permanently. We typically move in and out of a state of "being down." It moves us deeply to anticipate the loss of what is meaningful in our lives —people, places, memories. Anticipating death brings on melancholy. It can't be any different.

This is not to say we *should* be depressed. It is simply to reaffirm the reality and naturalness of depression in our dying.

In Psalm 6, the psalmist cries out:

> Pity me, Yahweh, I have no strength left,
> heal me, my bones are in torment,
> my soul is in utter torment.
> Yahweh, how long will you be? . . .
> Every night I drench my pillow
> and soak my bed with tears;
> my eye is wasted with grief (JB).

Later in the same psalm, the psalmist says in relief:

> Yahweh has heard the sound of my weeping,
> Yahweh has heard my petition,
> Yahweh will accept my prayer.

There is light behind the dark clouds.

Read Psalm 22:1-24
      Psalm 43:5
      John 16:20-22

Here I am, Lord. I'm down and out, depressed.
I think I am in love with my own sadness.
Help me to fall out of love with it and in love
with my limited living. A little is a lot—help
me to see this. Amen.

love
The Eternal Hold

"Love makes the world go 'round," the song says. Love has been sung about, written about, analyzed, dissected for centuries. And love has had more done to it, for it, and through it than we can imagine.

Yet, what is love? I don't know what it means to you. You'd have to tell me. It means different things for different people. And it remains largely a mystery for all of us, never completely understood or consistently experienced.

Paul saw love as "the greatest." Jesus put love at the heart of the two great commandments. No doubt, we need it. Life can't be fulfilling without it. What about love for the dying? You tell me!

Billy Jean said that it was the love she knew with her husband and children that helped her in dying. Without that, she didn't know what she would have done. At the same time, she said love also brought her pain. She was about to lose these loved ones, and this hurt deeply. She said, though, that she would rather hurt this way than not have known their love. "On the other side of my hurt is a fire that destroys that pain and gives me warmth. Our love is that kind of warm fire."

Herb said that if it weren't for the love of his family, he didn't know how he would have survived as long as he had. His love for his family had a great deal to do with his struggle to survive.

What does love mean to us? Perhaps it's intimacy, a closeness we experience but can't accurately describe. Perhaps it's knowing that our family will be cared for. Perhaps it's friends who relate honestly and warmly, who help us put things in order and bring us what we want and need. Perhaps it's that special person who says little, but simply is there, with us, in our dying. Perhaps it's our neighbor who is taking good care of our pet. Perhaps it's the kind words and gentle touch of a nurse, an aide, a technician, a doctor. Perhaps it's the concern conveyed by a physician, a pastor. Perhaps it's the way a friend helps us eat. Perhaps it's sharing memories with someone who lived them with us. Love is acted and felt it various ways.

However we come to know it, it's "the greatest."

The Bible uses the Greek word *agape*, that unconditional, self-giving love totally intent on the one to whom it is given. This love, without strings attached, we may know in part. It is fully known in Christ, and offered to us.

As Arlyce approached death, she said, "It's funny, that old children's hymn keeps coming to me. I even find myself humming it spontaneously. 'Jesus loves me, this I know, for the Bible tells me so.' I know he loves me. The Bible tells me, but I've also experienced it."

Read Romans 8:31-39
       Ephesians 3:14-21
       1 John 4:7-12

O Love that will not let me go,
I rest my weary soul in thee;
I give thee back the life I owe,
That in thine ocean depths its flow
May richer, fuller be.
                    —*George Matheson*

solitude

Leave Me Alone

There come moments, hours, longer periods of time when we just want to be alone. We feel a deep need to withdraw from people, places, whatever is close, familiar, loving. We want to get away.

When we feel the grip of death approaching, we may pull back and seek solitude. Something inside tells us that when all is said and done, when death's grip finally tightens, we really are alone. Perhaps this parallels the aloneness of birth. Though we were surrounded by a physician and nurses, we came into the world alone. In the beginning, we are alone; in the end, we are alone. And we may choose isolation as death approaches.

Sandra felt bad. She needed to reduce the intense press of loved ones around her. She was tired of talking, entertaining, even of being realistically serious with those who were straightforward with her. But it was difficult and painful for her to say, "I want to be alone." She was caught between her love for friends and family and a surging need for solitude. She thought she was being cool when she told them to go away. She was afraid they would think she no longer cared for them, that she had become callous, uncaring, perhaps even that she'd "flipped." Sometimes, when communication faltered, her words did sound harsh, cold, angry. Sandra feared people would feel rejected. In spite of this, she took the risk, and she was glad.

All of us need to recognize the need to pull back, to be alone. We may fear remaining isolated. This isn't an unreasonable fear, since it might occur. But if we don't permit the risk, whose need would we be meeting? For Sandra, isolation was temporary.

On occasion Jesus withdrew from people, even from his closest friends. He withdrew to think, to meditate, to commune with God and his own soul. Before his death, at the Garden of Gethsemane, he withdrew to pray. He needed solitude as much as he needed his friends. On the cross he was truly alone—yet in relationship to the God who was, is, and shall be. "Into your hands I commend my spirit."

Read Matthew 14:22-23
       John 16:32-33

Dear God, there are times I need to be alone. You know me and my need. Help me to let my people know that I still love them, but I just need to be alone. If they don't understand, grant me courage to bear with the tension. If they do understand, help me give them my thanks. Amen.

acceptance
Yes, Me!

Rose Ann was dying. She knew it and was angry about it. Anger was the overriding theme of her dying. With anger, she seemed to preserve whatever energy and fight she had. At the same time, her anger kept almost everyone at a safe distance, leaving her in lonely isolation. She died angry, alone, not even resigned. Perhaps she died much like she had lived. Acceptance was beyond her grasp.

In all discussions about "dying with dignity," the stage of acceptance is considered essential to our finally being reconciled to our death. Yet not all people achieve this. Not all people want it. Many die without ever accepting their mortality.

Some people talk about being resigned to death. Resignation seems to mean giving in or giving up, which is vastly different from the acceptance that brings understanding and peace. Acceptance, more than anything else, frees a person to really live with dying. It is the bridge between despair and hope.

Acceptance is also a gift the dying person leaves to the loved survivors. "I know that Emily accepted her death. Her acceptance has helped me to go on living. She wanted it that way."

I entered Joe's room for the first time. He had cancer. According to his family, no one had told him. He was expected to die that very day. His speech was garbled and difficult to understand, but toward the end of our strained conversation came these clear words: "My suitcase is packed."

Joe knew, even though no one had told him. He was ready to die, packed and ready. Half an hour after our conversation, he died. Even though his family lived with the guilt of their denial, Joe left them an imperishable gift—his acceptance.

Acceptance isn't easy. I find it hard even to accept the fact that I get sick. It interferes with my living. I like to believe that I am so healthy and all-powerful that I am immune from disease and accidents.

News of impending death is the ultimate reminder of my lack of control over life. Death is the ultimate loss, and accepting it is a struggle. We all struggle in our own way. Acceptance comes with more or less difficulty or not at all, depending on who we are and what we believe.

Jesus spoke to his disciples a number of times about his future death. They couldn't accept it. Still, Jesus spoke of it and struggled for himself. He sweat drops like blood in the garden. He struggled with God's will and his acceptance. In the end, he showed us what acceptance is. "Father, into thy hands I commit my spirit." "It is finished."

Read Genesis 48:21
       Genesis 49:28-33
       2 Corinthians 6:1-2

Dear Father, acceptance of my dying and my death is a struggle. One day I feel that I am being realistic and the next day I want to hide or run away. Thank you for being with me in the struggle. You give me courage and hope. Amen.

hope
A New Day

I've never seen anyone rob another person of hope. We continually hope unless we have given up, and not many people do. Even feelings of despair give way to resurgent moments of hope.

We never lose the need for hope. Most, if not all, people maintain hope, even to death. We may reach acceptance of our dying but we still hope. It may be hope in a medication or treatment that will bring not just relief, but cure. It may be hope in fulfilling one more personal dream or in seeing a loved one's next important step in their life journey—graduation, marriage, a job, becoming a grandparent.

For the dying person, many factors gnaw away at hope—especially negative and pessimistic talk. Sally said, "It's depressing and discouraging to listen to the possible side effects and predicted outcomes of my disease. Sometimes I think medical people set us up to think and expect the worst. If I dwelled on that, I'd lose hope. I'd lose any motivation to deal positively with myself and this disease."

Being overly optimistic, on the other hand, creates false hope. Both extremes hurt and hinder more than they help. Each of us wrestles to maintain a balanced hope that is reasonable and helpful.

Physicians know the importance of hope and refuse to give exact predictions of death. This isn't a cover-up. They know they've been wrong too many times to predict accurately in every situation. Hope penetrates and disrupts medical predictions.

Allen said he got angry with and then felt sorry for those relatives and friends who told him he would be OK or not to worry. Some kept reminding him that miracles do happen. Their insistence reinforced the part of Allen's hope that denied reality. Allen said he didn't need depressing sad sacks with long faces and "ain't-it-awful" written all over their actions and words. He said, "I need people to be real with me, to hear the hopes and *fears* I have, and the way I live with these."

Then there was Elvera, who said simply, "Sure, I want to live. But don't forget, pastor, my hope is in the Lord. Whether I live or die, I'm with him." Her gentle reminder serves to point to the ultimate source of our hopes and to the ultimate hope. If home is where the heart is, it is both with our loved ones on earth and with our Father in heaven.

Read Psalm 16:9-11
      Psalm 42:11
      Romans 8:22-25
      Romans 15:13
      Colossians 1:22-23

My hope is in you, O Lord, who made heaven, earth, me, and all those important people in my life. Help me balance my hold on hope, not to tip into giving up and not to tip into denying my dying. Give me a heart that keeps you the center of my hope. Amen.

peace
A Spiritual High

When in war, we seek peace. When at peace, we seek to preserve the peace. We realize there is both need for outer peace—among nations, tribes, families, spouses—and need for inner peace, a feeling of harmony and contentment. In fact, the longing for peace is so prized that a whole subculture has been created to pursue it: the drug culture. Peace is indeed a prized possession.

In research about "life after life" experiences, one common theme has been an experience of peace. Some people who have been near death describe their out-of-body experiences with such words as "joy" and "peace." Christians talk about "the peace that passes understanding." Peace is a sought-for ideal. For some people, peace is also a deeply experienced reality.

In dying, peace comes as a result of acceptance. Words cannot accurately describe this spiritual high. As Rudy said, "I can't tell you what this peace exactly is. It is not something I believe. It is something I know." Such peace is indeed beyond our understanding.

Alice said it pained her to see that her family couldn't accept her dying. She said, "I know I really can't expect them to experience the peace I know, not now. Maybe after I die they will begin to understand. I have been able to reach out to them and help them. My peace has helped me to do this."

Peace moved Alice beyond herself. When we are not troubled or afraid, we are able to move out toward others. If they ask how this can be, we might say, as Maxine did, "I know God is with me and I am at peace."

This points us to the source of peace. Jesus said, "Peace I leave with you; my peace I give to you; not as the world gives do I give to you. Let not your hearts be troubled, neither let them be afraid" (John 14:27).

The wisdom of the ages, the history of centuries, and, most importantly, the message of the Bible clearly says there is a peace that goes beyond understanding. We can find peace in living—and in dying—through our Lord and Savior, Jesus Christ.

Read Psalm 121
       Romans 15:13
       Philippians 4:4-7

Dear God, you are the giver of every good and great gift. Help me to know your gift of peace and to share it with those who doubt and seek. Amen.

machines and things
Tubes, Bags, and Bleeps

"I saw that respirator once, and to think I might have to depend on that machine to breathe for me, I, I. . . ."

"Well, I'm thankful for all the know-how, but I wonder if I'll be able to die naturally, or if the machines will have the final word."

"Chemotherapy has given me some time, but it's taken its toll, too."

"Have you ever had to be hooked up to a Foley? I can take a lot, but not being able to go to the toilet, that's too much. It really gets to me."

"After a while, when I'm in cobalt, the tech and I don't know what to say. That table is always so hard. I feel like Startrek's plaything."

Machines and things help and hinder, shorten and prolong dying. We need them and we don't. We want them and we wish them away.

Tim knew he was dying, and he was ready. He said he wanted to die. His family didn't like him saying this openly, so he kept quiet most of the time. Shortly before his death he was put on a respirator. He tore the tube out. Some people said he was out of his mind, disoriented. They tied his arms to the bed. After another week, Tim finally died, in spite of the restraints and technology. Tim was clear about his readiness to die—but we weren't ready to let him.

On the other hand, Sophie was grateful for the machines and drugs that intervened in her medical crisis and pulled her through, giving her a little more time before her death.

Who's to say what is best, right, appropriate? There are no absolutely right and wrong answers to difficult medical questions. Each of us has thoughts, feelings, values, beliefs, desires, and we may want to clearly indicate what these are. More than likely, we'll have to insist on being heard rather than waiting for someone to ask us.

Irene knew her heart was in bad shape. What really miffed her was that, if she went into cardiac arrest again, her family wouldn't be allowed to be with her. She said, "They'll be pounding on my chest or zapping me with those heart zappers to get me going again. I just want my family close to me. That's what's important."

Everyone will not necessarily agree with what we decide, but we have a right to make our own decisions about dying, with or without majority opinion behind us. If we're capable of making our decision, we can decide to do everything, nothing, something. We may have to grab an arm or write a note to get the attention of those who care for us.

But we should be heard. Machines and things are here to serve us, not for us to serve them. We can take control if we want to.

As Eloise, age 78, said, "I don't want them to stick me full of tubes and hook me up and knock me out with drugs. I want to experience my own death. It's mine, you know!"

Read Ecclesiastes 3:1-8
        Psalm 43
        1 Corinthians 15:54-57
        1 Peter 3:13-17

My Lord, we have such medical sophistication. I appreciate much of it. It's helped me. But, Lord, help me and the people who care for me to know when enough is enough. Amen.

sexuality
Sex Isn't a Four-Letter Word

Sexuality covers a wide range of intimate and loving acts, from hugging to sexual intercourse. Denial of sexual needs may generate feelings of loneliness, abandonment, and depression. Dr. Stephen P. Hush, National Institute of Mental Health, reported at the Second National Conference of Human Value and Cancer that one of the biggest myths surrounding cancer is denial of the patient's sexual needs. In a pioneering program at the National Cancer Institute in Washington, D.C., married patients are allowed conjugal visits with their spouses and parents are permitted to sleep in the same bed with their sick children.

Jamie's appearance was always important to her. She spent a fair amount of time primping in front of a mirror to make sure that her hair and makeup were just right, so she could look like a million bucks. Usually, she did. She was an attractive woman and she worked to maintain her attractiveness.

Jamie was happily married, and she and her husband had a good sexual relationship. But she still enjoyed flirting and receiving other men's attention. She knew she was attractive, but occasionally she experienced uncertainty, since she didn't like herself quite as much as other people thought. She handled these doubts through primping, flirting, and vying for attention.

At 38, Jamie was dying. Some attractive people eventually give in to disease and lose all concern for their attractiveness and sexual activity, but Jamie's image and her need for attention were primary. During her dying she took even more care with her appearance. She tried not to be seen without one of her attractive hairpieces, and she took time for makeup, even when she needed someone to help her.

Jamie's husband didn't believe, as some people do, that the disease was catching. Their genital sexual relationship continued until Jamie was physically incapable. At that point, holding, stroking, hugging, kissing were all, and they were enough.

It's hard to feel sexy when your silky nightgown gives way to a hospital gown, that wraparound apron that's always flying open in the back. And if disease drastically alters your body, you may develop a negative image of your physical self. Our society's premium on beauty may cause you to doubt that you are still a sexual person. But sexuality is one of God's great gifts to you, and, as philosophers have said for years, beauty is in the eye of the beholder.

Oscar's bones seemed to pop out of his skin. His face was thin and sunken. He had little energy and strength. But when Oscar grinned, that frail body and wasted face came alive, and he was a beautiful human being.

In dying, we don't become sexless. For some people, sexuality and sexual expression become less important, but many continue to enjoy their sexuality. Much depends on what your sexuality meant to you before you learned you were going to die. If it has been important, it need not be less so now. You may need to make some changes and adjustments, but don't try to ignore the fact that you are still a sexual person with needs and desires.

Read Genesis 1:27
        Psalm 139:13-18
        1 Corinthians 6:20
        1 John 4:7

O God, in your Son Jesus you saw us for what we are—fully human. Look upon me now with love. Help me maintain my full humanity as I die, including my sexual self. Thank you. Amen.

eternal life
Timelessness

Did you ever wonder what it would be like to experience timelessness, to have no sense of a big hand and a small hand whirling away seconds, minutes, hours, while the calendar marks off day, month, year?

Little children come close to having no sense of time. Two of my boy's favorite time numbers were 4 and 14, which he used indiscriminantly to refer to minutes or hours. But children soon learn that yesterday and tomorrow are different from "now."

As adults our awareness of time is acute. We measure our very life and death with time. Sometimes we sense timelessness in dreams or fantasies, when time seems to stand still or be irrelevant. Going through surgery or emerging from a state of unconsciousness leaves us with a sense of time loss. We passed through time without recollection, as if it didn't happen. Some people who have been near death and believed they were in a realm of the spirit say that time seemed unimportant.

This sudden move from time to the eternal happens in the twinkling of an eye. Whatever may be on the other side of death, we believe God is eternally present. All will be changed and made new. Time may indeed be irrelevant. It won't preoccupy us as it does now. One second may be as one year.

Lottie said she was looking forward to an eternity with God and her loved ones. She said some people thought that would be pretty boring, but she didn't. She believed that when time became meaningless, her relationships to God and other people would be radically changed. What might be a drag now in time would be heaven then without time. Lottie was convinced!

Another concept of the eternal is continual relationship with what and who is good and meaningful. No one knows what the specifics are, but we envision a state of closeness and relationship which is unbroken, whole. While living on earth we seldom glimpse such wholeness. We occasionally know it in part, but then we will know in full.

Walter called it home. The eternal was the

"home above and beyond all homes, an eternal home." This was enough, for it was really all.

At a point close to death, Evie dreamed that Jesus came to her, picked her up from her bed, and carried her into a bright, warm light. Evie no longer fears death. She believes that when the time comes, she will be home, with Jesus.

Read John 11:26
      John 14:1-7

O God, I don't like leaving the people I love, the home I've known, the pleasure of living, but I look forward to the home that holds everything I love together more completely than I can imagine. Grant me your eternal home. Amen.

humor

A Little Dab Will Do Ya

Arnold had a complaint. People who knew he was dying no longer treated him like the old Arnold they always knew and loved. Arnold liked a good joke, even a bad joke now and then, but there wasn't much joking now that he was sick.

Sometimes, when I'm with a person who is in a prolonged dying process, other people in the room seem unsure whether they should even smile, let alone share some humor.

Humor is a wonderful gift. Sometimes it is used to avoid reality, to stifle feelings and deny the seriousness of the situation. But often humor can both buffer reality and illuminate it. It can be a way of sharing personal warmth and caring, making it easier for us to live together.

Will was being fed by IV. During the holidays he would point to the tube and say, "This is my turkey and stuffing and mashed potatoes!"

Marlene wore a wig, but there was no denying she was losing her hair. "I hope God does have every hair of my head numbered," she said with a grin. "It won't be long till I'll be able to count them myself—all one of them!"

Frieda lived longer than anyone expected. She would say, "I'm an ornery old cuss, and God doesn't want to take me to heaven while I'm so ornery!"

Humor is a gift to help us with our dying. It can be a way of reaching out and asking to be touched, to be regarded as a person. An entertainer who was dying said he hoped people realized that he was a human being, not just a star. But he still wanted to give to people what he had always tried to give—a little song, a little dance, and some humor to bring a smile to their face.

Sam said he found some people so remorseful when they tried to talk to him that he would crack a joke to see if he could lift their spirits. "I have to do something—otherwise they'll get me down even if I'm feeling good!"

We all need smiles to lighten our heavy loads. As a children's song says, "A smile is just a frown turned upside down." A smile won't take all our troubles away. Life isn't that simple. But many a dying spirit still wants and needs to laugh.

Read Proverbs 17:22
        John 16:33

Lord, sometimes my laughter gets swallowed up in my pain, my sadness, my anger. Help me, O God, to smile, to laugh. Give wings of gladness to my heart. Amen.

priorities

Taking Stock

Have you ever said that you've collected so much stuff that you're running out of room? Did you vow to sort through everything, one thing at a time, and keep only what's necessary and important?

People take stock of their clothes closets, garages, basements, attics. But how often do we take stock of our lives?

When we realize we are dying, our priorities change. The knowledge of approaching death colors our attitudes, feelings, beliefs. It may prompt us to seriously take stock of what's important to us. Is it money, hobbies, a special painting or book, unresolved issues, friends, family, God?

Jody was surprised and irritated with people's tendency to get upset over what she saw as rather small matters. She said she could understand, because she'd been the same way, but now that she was dying, she saw how much she'd missed by devoting energy to trivial things. She'd let unimportant things divert her from what mattered. "How often I was cross with the children, and how seldom I simply told them I loved them!"

What is important? When I was healthy it was. . . . Now that I'm dying it is. . . .

Wilbert had been separated from his daughter by mutual choice. She was in her twenties and working in another city. Disagreements had created tension between them and they'd always had a difficult time talking, but they did love each other. When Wilbert was dying, they both wanted to be reconciled, to forgive each other and express their love. They couldn't. They sat and talked, but not about their heart's deep desires. Tragically, they were immobilized. They couldn't break through the old barriers and share their feelings about what was important.

Dea said she realized now how important God was to her. She'd always been fairly active in church, but she hadn't really given God much thought. But now she had a dream in which she felt God's presence so strongly that she knew God was with her. That was enough.

On the cross, Jesus took stock. His words tell

us what was important to him. He asked John to look after his mother. He responded to the thief with the gift of salvation. He lifted his spirit to his Father. What is important to you?

Read John 19:25-27
        1 Peter 4:7-11

O God, whether I deliberately decide or not, I am choosing what is really important. Guide my thoughts and feelings as I take stock. Amen.

time

Minutes Feel Like Hours, Hours Feel Like Minutes

Time is both partner and enemy. It is both praised and cursed. We want more of it when we have little. We want less of it when we have too much.

Otto recalled how his previous hospital stays had driven him wild. He had known few limitations in his life, but in the hospital he was restricted, and he hated it. His minutes felt like hours. Time was an enemy.

Now Otto is dying, going downhill quickly. The time that once moved so slowly is now moving faster than Otto wants. The hours feel like minutes, precious minutes.

We've all heard people say that it's not how much time we have, but what we do with it that counts. There's great truth in that. Yet, unless the physical and mental pain becomes

too great, most of us want just a little more time.

Nevertheless, it's much more productive to concentrate on making the most of the time we have. Well-spent minutes can be rich and full. We remember these famous words: "I shall pass through this world but once. If, therefore, there be any kindness I can show, or any good thing I can do, let me do it now; let me not defer it or neglect it, for I shall not pass this way again" (Etienne de Grellet).

Dying confronts us with our stewardship of time. With no extra hours to fritter away, we want to devote our time to what's important. Tillie said the most important things for her were reading her Bible and talking with her family and a few select friends. She decided that was the best use she could make of her time. She made sure she used her time the way she wanted, until time one day stood still.

Josh said he was going to read all those books he had always wanted to read. He got a good start.

Cal knit winter stocking hats. Half the hospital seemed to be wearing them and buying them. He proudly displayed the many colors and styles. "Gotta feel useful," he'd say.

In many ways time measures and masters us throughout our life's journey. But we can measure and master time with our positive attitude and by our determination to use our time well. After all, time is neutral. Whether it is for us or against us is really up to us.

"The hour has come." "Could you not wait with me one hour?" Jesus knew and used time. His acceptance of time is summed up in those final words, "It is finished." Time as we know it ends, but timelessness begins—an eternity with our God.

Read Psalm 90
       Ecclesiastes 3:1-8
       2 Corinthians 6:1-2

Dear God, time hasn't always been my friend. Help me to befriend it. And thank you for my special memories of all those occasions when time has been my friend. Amen.

pills and pain
The Perilous Ps

Charlene said the hardest thing for her was the pain. It could be controlled, but not completely. It could even be eliminated at times, but it always came back.

Conrad didn't mind the pain as much as the pills. "I'm afraid I'll get addicted, or I'll be so doped up that I'll lose my mind and be completely dependent."

Pills and pain are usually part of dying. How should we deal with them?

If we take pills long enough, we start to call them by their colors and what they're supposed to do. We also become counters: "I'm up to six now. I started with two." It is difficult to know how many pills are necessary for each of us to deal with pain, to get to sleep, to increase our appetite. If you have seldom taken medication, a small amount may do the job. On the other hand, you may need more to do the same job that a little has done for someone else. You can assist those who care for you by letting them know how many pills seem to be enough. You can control pills by telling your doctors, nurses, and family what works. This perilous p will become manageable if you take charge of it.

What about the other perilous p—pain? Much controversy surrounds pain. Psychological research shows that it is increased by anxiety and depression. Physical pain can be "more painful" because of your psychological and spiritual condition.

Raymond seemed to talk constantly about his pain. People stayed with him only a few minutes. They performed their tasks and left.

Then Goldie, a volunteer, decided to spend some time with Raymond. She sat by his bed. He talked about his pain. She stayed. She came back. Within a few days, he began to talk less about his pain. He began to share his life with Goldie—memories, disappointments, fantasies.

Raymond's pain hadn't gone away. Occasionally he still mentioned it. But when Raymond found someone who cared enough to listen, he found better things to talk about than his pain.

Pain affects the whole of us. We can draw on

physical, psychological, and spiritual resources to manage it, cooperating with medical people, counselors, pastors, and loved ones. Talking and praying are at least as important as medications. And there are a host of new and experimental methods for dealing with pain, such as meditation and feedback techniques.

Pain is a burden, but it is also a teacher. It provides messages about our attitudes and the way we relate to others. Do we let our fear of pain do us more harm than the pain itself? Do we see ourselves as martyrs, long-suffering heroes? Or do we allow pain to help us recognize our physical limitations and show us that we are part of a suffering human family?

If you have to live with pain, learn how to manage it. Don't let it dull your human spirit. Pray for strength. And remember these words: "My grace is sufficient for you, for my power is made perfect in weakness" (2 Cor. 12:9).

Read Job 33:19-28
        Hebrews 5:7-9
        Revelation 21:2-4

Dear God, in my times of pain, nourish my spirit. Even when my body fails, may I realize you have not failed me. Amen.

fear
Night Shadows

With the night-light on, shadows would form on the bedroom wall. My little daughter would say, "Shadows, Dad. What are they?" Then I'd ask her what they looked like. Answers ranged from "shadows" to "rectangles" to "alligators"!

The night-light was a comfort, providing security in the darkness. But the shadows from the light were frightening. Together we explored them, touched them, talked about them. This reduced the demon fear lurking in those mysterious shadows.

Fear is a strange and paradoxical emotion. It sometimes is positive, since it alerts us to danger and often compels us to take action.

Phyllis noticed a little lump in her breast. At first she said, "It's a gland," and, "I'll wait awhile. It'll probably go away." It didn't. She was aware of warning signs of cancer and the need for an immediate checkup, but she waited, her fear mounting. Finally she saw a doctor. Fear motivated her to be actively concerned about her health.

But fear can also be negative. Bonaro W. Overstreet, in his book *Understanding Fear in Ourselves and Others,* says:

> Of all the emotional forces that pattern our individual and interpersonal behaviors, fear has the most insidious power to make us do what we ought not to do and leave undone what we ought to do. Under its influence and trying to escape its influence, we seem fated to give it a yet stronger hold upon us.

What part does fear play as we deal with our terminal illness and our relationship to loved ones and to God? It can get a demon hold on us—but there are ways to loose its hold. Clara said, "It took some work and lots of talking, but I'm not so afraid anymore." She had been running from her worst fears, but when she realized how much energy it took to run and how futile it was, she reversed the energy and faced her fears. She'd been afraid to admit she was dying and afraid to discuss personal tensions with family members. Then she risked facing her death, risked confronting her family members. Not all family tensions were eliminated, but their intensity was reduced. Clara's fear was lowered and became manageable. She took charge of it instead of letting it take charge of her.

Alex said he had no fear of dying. "I gave it to God and God helped me. After all, God needed something to do too, and what better helper?"

Jesus often said, "Be not afraid." With his help, we can chase away the night shadows of fear.

Read Psalm 34:4
      Isaiah 12:2-3
      Mark 4:35-41
      Hebrews 2:14-15

When at last I near the shore,
And the fearful breakers roar
Twixt me and the peaceful rest,
Then, while leaning on thy breast,
May I hear thee say to me:
"Fear not, I will pilot thee."
                    —Edward Hopper

loss of control

Who's in Charge Here?

Rudy had always prided himself on being independent and making his own decisions. In the hospital he felt his independence slipping away, and he was frustrated and angry. He said, "Sometimes they seem to think I can't decide anything. Even the doctors act like I don't know what's going on or can't figure it out."

George felt the same way: "People standing over me, talking down to me, over me, through me. People willing to do anything for me, even things I can do for myself. I feel diminished, like I've lost some of me, my I-ness, who I am, especially when I'm not involved in decisions that affect me. It's like being annihilated as a person."

Rudy and George were protesting the loss

of independence that may accompany dying and hospitalization. We lose our freedom of movement when we are confined to a bed, a room, a wheelchair. And the freedom to make decisions may also be narrowed or lost.

Unlike Rudy and George, Ken didn't want to be in control. He withdrew into self-pity and became sullen and distant.

We may not always like the responsibility of making decisions, yet we are used to making them. To have that indicator of our freedom and self-respect taken away may seem to be the final insult.

"I didn't decide to die," cried Jessie. "Nobody is going to take away my right to make my own decisions in my dying."

Intent on "being Jessie," she made sure she had a say in decisions, and she continued to do as much for herself as physically possible. Even when she could no longer care for herself, she kept giving the orders!

Fern's doctor explained to her family that surgery would not cure her, but it might prolong her life. Without consulting Fern, the family told the doctor they approved of the surgery and were certain that Fern would agree. When Fern learned what had happened, she was angry. It became painfully clear to all that the family had violated her integrity as a feeling, thinking person capable of making her own decisions.

The ability to choose gives meaning to our living and our dying. At times we may be tempted to turn over our lives to a hospital, a doctor, a spouse, our family. But if we do, we run the risk of forfeiting a degree of our humanity, and our spirit will be diminished.

None of us wants to be a tyrant, making constant demands on the medical staff or on loved ones. But we need enough control over what is happening to us and around us so that we can feel like respected and responsible human beings.

Suzanne took the bull by the horns. She informed her doctor that she wanted to know what was happening to her, that he shouldn't hide anything. She asked him to try his best to explain everything simply, without highfalutin medical language. "I'll forgive you if it isn't easy," she said, "but not if you don't try!" She said she wouldn't promise not to cry or get angry, but she believed she'd get through it. She added, "Before you ask my family to decide something, as long as I've got my mind, you talk to me or all of us together." Here was a woman who took nothing for granted and wasn't afraid of people in high places. She treasured her ability to decide.

George said to the nursing assistant, "Say, I

never had my bath at 10:00 A.M. at home. How 'bout us working out something so I can get it in the evening like I always did? I know it messes up order and routine here." Then, with a sly grin, he added, "Call it a dying man's last request." This was George's way to preserve his freedom to decide, feel human, and grin in the teeth of death.

The apostle Peter died a martyr. Of the stories surrounding his death, one says that he asked to be crucified head-downward because he didn't presume to be equal to his Lord. This was Peter's way of expressing humility, honor, devotion, and love for Jesus. Peter maintained his soul-freedom to the end, deciding his very posture in death. With this he claimed his human dignity.

Read Proverbs 3:21-26
         Proverbs 25:28

O God, I want to make my own decisions. Sometimes I'm too afraid or too upset. Give me the energy and confidence to take control of my dying, and to do what is best, day to day, moment to moment. I need to know your presence and strength is at work in me. Amen.

faith

Caught for Eternity

Some people seem to have no doubt about keeping their faith while they live and when they die. Others have always struggled with this thing called faith. Some fear they may lose their faith when the going gets tough, particularly when the going leads smack-dab into a dead end—death.

In *Free Fall*, a dying person's human, beautiful book, JoAnn Kelley Smith tells what faith means to her:

> Although I have found little help from the Scriptures to tell me what my life after death will be, I know it will be different. Even as the resurrected Jesus had changed so that he was not readily identified—so it will be with me. For me, that belief is a leap of faith. The first leap I made was to

give my life to God in this present life. That was an act of faith. And when you decide you are going to be God's person and not your own, you really don't know where that is going to take you or what you are going to do or where you are going to be. . . . Dying, in my best understanding after these many months, is that time when I take my second leap of faith. It's a part of the free fall—like the trapeze artist high above the crowd who suddenly falls. And seemingly from nowhere with split-second timing, his partner below swings out, reaches out, catches him, and saves him. That leap of faith is when I take my last conscious breath. In faith, I believe God will reach out and catch me.

A thief on a cross asked that Jesus remember him. Jesus said, "Today you will be with me in Paradise." In mid-air there was reaching out. A thief took a leap of faith and was caught for eternity.

Not everyone experiences such a sudden change of heart, a dramatic leap of faith. Roslyn said she had always believed. Even in her bad times, she somehow just knew God would be with her. No matter what, God cared. When Roslyn found out she had inoperable cancer, her world fell apart. She struggled. Yet she moved along her journey toward death with words echoing the Roslyn of old. "I've really had the big one thrown at me! This isn't the first, but I know it's the last. You know, I still know God's with me. Now that may sound strange to you, but I've had faith he was with me from the beginning, and we're sure not letting go of each other now!"

JoAnn Kelley Smith, a thief on a cross, Roslyn, you and I, we all have a mustard seed of faith—and it will be enough!

Read Isaiah 12:2
       John 20:26-31
       Romans 5:1-2
       Hebrews 11:1-16

Dear Father, sometimes my faith seems like a light grown dim. Sometimes my faith seems like a light grown bright. Sometimes I experience darkness. Help me to know, through light and darkness, that your grasp is sure. Amen.

suicide

It's Crossed My Mind

Trevor had been an outgoing, successful, proud man. Now his condition was deteriorating, and he knew there was no known cure. He felt his advance toward death was robbing him of all he had been, and he couldn't seem to discover what else he might be. He found himself becoming impatient with his friends. He was rough on the hospital staff, and he snapped at his wife and children. Trevor wanted to be numbed into oblivion. He wanted to die.

As death draws near, many people are impatient for the end. Aggie was blind and wasting. She asked her pastor to pray a special prayer—that soon she would die.

Some people, weary of waiting, think, "Why drag this out any longer? Why not kill myself?" We know that some people commit suicide when they realize they are dying. Friends sometimes help the dying take their lives.

Bob told his wife about his suicidal thoughts, but he also assured her that he wouldn't kill himself. He loved life and wanted what time he had left. At the same time, he insisted that his life not be prolonged unnecessarily. He wrote down his wishes and made all the arrangements. He wasn't going to commit suicide, but he wouldn't let technology drag out his dying.

Christians are often greatly distressed that thoughts of suicide enter their minds. They try to dismiss them, shut them out, pretend they're not there. But it is normal for dying people to have such thoughts, and we can understand why they occur. We are struggling human beings, living with a death that will one day claim us. Having suicidal impulses doesn't make us bad or unchristian, and we need not feel guilty.

Noreen said, "Sometimes I wonder why I should keep fighting to live. I get exhausted and discouraged. In my low moments I think, why not end it all? Then someone comes to pass some time with me, and they really listen to what I'm saying. I discover a new book, or I remember the times I went skiing in the winter and swimming in the summer. I think about my children's laughter. I *do* want to live."

My son once planted a bean seed in a clay pot. He waited impatiently for it to sprout. It was so hard to wait, watch, and nurture that little seed. Finally, in his eagerness, he emptied out the pot.

Sometimes we're just as impatient as my son, and we want to take matters into our own hands. But hope pierces through impatience again and again, even as we die. We can be born daily, like a sunrise, until death comes. Then we can be born new, totally, once more.

Read Psalm 55:4-8
      Psalm 102:1-11
      Matthew 6:34
      Philippians 4:11-13

Dear Father, you know my thoughts, feelings, impulses, fantasies. You don't frighten easily. I give myself to your understanding and assurance. Amen.

communication
A Word about Words

How do you talk about what is happening to you? Dr. Elisabeth Kübler-Ross has pointed out that we have at least three ways of communicating about dying: nonverbally, and with indirect or direct words.

We all communicate nonverbally, whether we intend to or not. When he learned he was dying, Henry pulled all the shades and kept one dim light on. Jill held my hand tightly, slowly released it, then turned her back. These were powerful nonverbal messages about dying.

Some people speak in symbols. A worker in a nursing home said that residents would talk about coming in the front door and going out the back.

Some people use plain English. I was stunned

by a man I'd just met who said, "I don't want to beat around the bush. I'm dying."

Many of us find this difficult. Even in a hospital we sometimes have a hard time using plain English. We talk diagnosis, avoiding the issue of death by focusing on medical details. We say, "He's not doing well" instead of "He's dying."

Jack said, "Some people talk straight with me and treat me like they always did, but some of them are scared. They act like all of a sudden I'm a different person, somebody they don't know. They're uncomfortable and don't know what to say. And then there are the people who think they're doing me a favor by keeping the truth from me. They don't want to hurt me by talking openly, but they end up hurting me more. I *need* to talk about my dying."

Have you found someone to talk to? Deep down, all of us need to communicate. But lines of communication, like muscles, need to be exercised if they're to be in good shape. If you're not used to discussing your important thoughts and feelings, you may well find it difficult to discuss your dying. But you need to talk in some way, both to understand and to be understood.

You have a unique opportunity to help others learn and grow. You can help people who haven't faced their own death become more comfortable in talking about dying. You can teach as no one else can, because you know what dying is like.

On her deathbed, Theresa decided to become an educator. Since she was dying and everyone around her wasn't, she could teach these healthy people about dying. Whenever anyone gave a hint of interest in her, she turned it into an opportunity to help that person learn to communicate with a dying person and to share thoughts and feelings about dying.

Not everyone is willing to listen to straight talk about death. Some hear, some don't. Some see, some are blind. You probably know who you can talk to. It may be your loved ones, but it may be someone else. If you persist, someone will quit trying to shut you up or tune you out. Someone will listen.

Read Proverbs 18:4, 21
       Proverbs 15:23
       Proverbs 25:11

*Dear God, you have given me the gift of
communicating. I'd like to wait for others
to be sensitive and start talking to me, but
maybe I'll have to break the ice myself. Help
me to melt them with my words. Amen.*

practical matters
Getting Your House in Order

My father has given my brother and me information he thinks will be helpful in handling the various responsibilities surrounding his death. This includes biographical information for his obituary and a description of the funeral service he wants, complete with his favorite hymns. He's told us where his important papers are and who's to be notified.

I'm grateful that he's taken charge and put things in order for us. My brother and I won't have to wonder if we're doing right by Dad. He's told us what he wants. This is his gift.

The old cliche about getting your house in order is based on wisdom. Jerry had handled all the financial matters in the family. When he learned he was dying, he began to teach his wife all about his insurance policies and important papers so she could take over. She struggled to learn, though it was painful, a constant reminder that Jerry was dying. This was an important house-ordering task for Jerry.

For Rod and Gretchen, getting the house in order involved more than finances and funeral arrangements. Would the children go to the funeral? Would Gretchen marry again? These issues were difficult to discuss, but they came to some positive, mutual decisions.

Getting the house in order means different things for each of us. Over a period of time, Elizabeth gradually gave away her most precious treasures to special people. Each person received a part of Elizabeth for a particular reason. Elizabeth was preparing them for her death as she brought order to her house.

Jesus shared a last meal with friends, made Peter aware of a depth of forgiveness he had never experienced before his denial, assured the disciples of his reality after his death, and sent the Spirit through which they were to know God. He prepared them and put his house in order.

Read Genesis 49
        Matthew 16:21-23
        Matthew 17:22-23

*Dear Father, I need to put my house in order.
About the time I think I have, something
else pops up. Give me patience and per-
sistence. And when I've finished, give me
a sense of assurance that I've done well.
Thank you. Amen.*

parting
Such Sweet Sorrow

Birth itself is a separation, and from birth on our lives are filled with goodbyes and partings. The French have a saying: *Partir, c'est mourir un peu.* It means, "To say goodbye is to die a little" or "Parting is a little death."

One person said, "I don't want to think about that. I'll get down and start feeling terrible!" Yet, thinking about our separations may help us face the process of dying, which leads to the final separation, death.

Do you like goodbyes? I haven't met anyone who does, unless of course they want to be rid of a certain person. Goodbyes involving people we love are hard.

When my family and I visit my parents, we enact what I call an eternal goodbye as we drive away, waving and honking continually until they are completely out of sight. We are reluctant to let go, to really say goodbye, to turn our backs and leave. To say goodbye is to die a little. We really may not see each other again. That goodbye thought is the hardest one.

Dying is a process of separation that we all handle in our own ways. Alex walked into the intensive care unit, where his dad lay unconscious. Alex stayed eight feet from the bed. He never moved any closer. Distance and separation had characterized their life together. Now it expressed Alex's denial and fear of his father's death.

Arden had a sign put on his door: "No visitors, only immediate family." He didn't need isolation for medical reasons, but he wanted to be left alone. Goodbyes were difficult for him, reminders that he was dying. In the end, he didn't want his family to be there either. He asked them to go home and rest. They did, and that night he died.

Sharon wanted all her immediate family with her as death approached. Even though separation was imminent, she preferred to be surrounded by those she loved and who loved her. She wanted to let go knowing what mattered most to her, her family, surrounded her in the final goodbye.

What we may sometimes forget in our goodbyes, partings, and separations is that not only do we lose something or someone, but we also receive and take something or someone with us. Even in our goodbyes, we die and we live.

Lorraine knew her death was just around the corner, but she was alert. She told her loved ones she wanted them to know that, in her parting, she was taking with her their love and care, her memories of beloved hymns and Mozart favorites, thoughts of the garden she loved, and a sense of the light and warmth of her favorite time of day—sunrise, which brought her hope for a new day.

To say goodbye is to die a little. To say goodbye is to embrace the possibility of a new day.

Read Psalm 139:1-12
        Romans 8:35-39

Dear Lord, parting can be such sweet sorrow.
Give me strength for the sorrow, and help
me to anticipate the sweetness. Amen.

grace

Something for Nothing

Carl Rogers, the elderly renowned clinical psychologist, has said that what most people are looking for is to be understood and accepted.

I know he's right. At particular moments in my life's journey, I have felt and continue to feel that what I want is someone who really understands and accepts me. Fortunately, I have known people who did understand and accept.

Grace, like love, is something Christians hear about and occasionally talk about. But, also like love, grace is sometimes difficult to realize and experience.

At times I find it difficult to be in the position of a receiver. I feel weak, helpless. I want to give, tit for tat. To "get something for nothing"

sounds good, but experiencing it may make us feel obligated. Yet most of us want unconditional understanding and acceptance, too — something for nothing, or better, something for just being ourselves.

Then again, some people feel so worthless or unforgivable, they can't believe they can be graciously forgiven and valued unless they pay a painful price, a price so great it's probably impossible to pay. We like to be able to say: "I did it on my own. I don't need anything."

Al had been a hard-working man who talked about pulling himself up by his own bootstraps. He was fiercely independent and proud of his accomplishments. But cancer didn't listen to Al. It took its toll. In a moment of reflection, Al talked about the difficulty of knowing and the need to know grace: "This cancer has me. This is the first time in my life I haven't been able to be in control, having it all my way. You know what's really tough—to let my family and friends be good to me, to accept me now, in this condition, when I can't ever repay them like I should."

Something for nothing, just because you are you. The graciousness of friends and relatives is a gift. God's grace is a gift. The only thing asked is that you receive. That isn't always easy. But if we allow ourselves to experience grace, we find it is beautiful beyond description. It is the warm smile of God that cuts through pain, self-pity, loneliness, anger, hurt, guilt, and fear, to say, "I accept you. I am yours and you are mine, no matter what."

Now may the grace of our Lord Jesus Christ, the love of God, and the communion of the Holy Spirit, be and abide with you forever. Amen.